MACROBIOTIC COOKING

By
Michele Cowmeadow

Published by

Cornish Connection
The Coach House, Buckyette Farm, Littlehempston,
Totnes, Devon TQ9 6ND

I would like to thank all the teachers of my life,
macrobiotic and otherwise. I would like to
thank the world for being as it is and those still
moments that arise unexpectedly and show me
with startling clarity what a beautiful universe
we have been given to live in.

First published May 1986
Fifth Edition April 1992

ISBN 0 948603 01 1

Contents

What is Macrobiotics?

Macrobiotics is more than a diet, it is a way of eating and living. There are so many aspects to macrobiotics as a way of life; essential macrobiotics is a way to achieve peace by regaining our individual health. Once we regain our health, of which one characteristic is understanding that we can help one another to live happily on this earth, we understand that we can recreate peace.

Once we eat whole grains and cut out meat and dairy foods then the fear and anger that cause hatred between people disappears. We can see that, as human beings, we are strongly connected with one another; the differences between us become smaller and smaller and we recognise that what we all wish for in life is alike; we want to love and be loved; we want to create friendships, have a happy family of bright and lively children and adults who encourage, trust and support each other deeply.

It is our individual commitment to creating a happy family that is the basis of a peaceful society.

Introduction to Macrobiotic Cooking

In order to achieve happiness as individuals we need to change our way of eating and understanding. The quality of our food should be the best available to us. Grains and vegetables should preferably be organic. The food we eat takes its energy from the soil it grows in and so it is important that the fertility of the soil is formed from the natural breakdown of rotting plant material rather than fertility being artificially produced by the addition of chemical fertilizers. Organic grains are stronger and more healing than chemicalised ones.

In the macrobiotic way of eating we choose to eat whole grains as much as possible. Whole grains give us a more wholistic and wholesome view of the world we live in, split grains and flour give us a more partial, a more refined view. Whole grains also give us more vitality because they revitalise our whole body.

It is good to cook joyfully and peacefully remembering how the food that we eat can make us, and those that share our food with us, happy or unhappy. So bring love into the making of your food and the recreation of your life.

When we begin the macrobiotic way of eating we have to relearn the quality of the foods that we eat and how they affect us physically, mentally and emotionally. To help us do this we use a conceptual tool of classifying foods by their yin or yang nature to help re-establish our native intuition about how different foods affect us. Yin and yang are always found together in different proportions in different foods.

In terms of cooking yin means lighter cooking, shorter cooking, more water and less salt. Yang, in terms of cooking refers to longer cooking, heavier cooking and greater use of fire and salt.

As we learn to understand and balance these two opposite tendencies in terms of the food we eat and the cooking styles we use, it is possible for us to become more healthy and enjoy more vitality from the food we eat.

Cooking is very important in creating our appetite for life. Gradually our food has lost its vitality because it is no longer natural. Our food is no longer natural because it has been refined. Our food has been increasingly more refined because our desire for the sensorial quality of these foods has never been satiated. If we return to using whole grains we return to a way of eating that has more life-giving energy in it.

Our cooking changes with the seasons. In the winter we want more long-cooked and warming foods because it is cold outside. In the summer we generally want shorter cooked and more watery foods because outside it is hot and dry.

In the summer, although we eat either a pressed or boiled salad with the occasional raw salad, we also make one longer cooked, more strengthening vegetable or protein dish each day so that we remain vital.

Winter days we like to eat long cooked stews, baked and long sauteed vegetables but we still need some really light foods each day, such as boiled salad and quick pickles, depending on our condition.

Root vegetables such as carrot and burdock are more warming, strengthening vegetables, round vegetables such as onion and cauliflower are very sweet- tasting and relaxing; leafy green vegetables such as spring greens, kale and spring onions are energising and cooling.

Whole grains form the central part of the macrobiotic diet because they are a very well balanced food. They contain very sustaining energy which lasts us easily between one meal and the next, if they are chewed well. Grains need to be chewed well before they are digestible. We use 50-60% whole grains every day. Most usually we eat rice with barley or rice with wheat, occasionally we cook rice with oats or dried corn. We use corn less often as a main grain because it is not strengthening enough. We tend generally to use buckwheat less often and more usually as a winter dish because it warms the body too much for most people living in this climate.

In the winter we eat comparatively more root vegetables and in the summer more leafy green vegetables, but throughout the year we eat some of each in each meal. This is natural; we are eating in harmony with foods as they ripen. The vegetable shop is filled with leafy greens in summer; watercress, Chinese cabbage and spring onions. In winter there is a greater variety of root and round vegetables; carrots, parsnips, turnips and swedes.

At first, cooking macrobiotically seems really difficult and time-consuming but gradually it becomes easier and more enjoyable. When you learn to cook rice and barley together well you will feel the benefits of eating whole grains. Miso soup is another food which gives us a lot more energy when we cook it well.

This book can help you learn to cook wholefoods but it is difficult to convey in writing how to make a balanced meal according to the macrobiotic way of eating. The best way to learn this sense of balance is from someone with a lot of experience in cooking this way.

To get a list of experienced cooking teachers in your area you can write to:- *The Macrobiotic Cooking Agency, 10, Netherleigh Close, Hornsey Lane, London N6 5LL. Telephone: 01 281 3235*

The Elements used in Cooking

Four elements have been used throughout the ages, by man, to transform raw food and make it more digestible by cooking.

The most obvious of these elements is fire which has a drying and yangizing effect on food. The best form of fire to use in cooking is wood, a relatively low energy (yang) fuel. Gradually we have discovered more powerful fuels; coal, oil, gas, and finally, electricity and atomic fuel (very yin).

We use fire to transform the acid content of yin, vegetable quality food, in order to ingest a more yang quality food. The more highly powered or yin energy sources, such as electricity or microwave, are much worse for our health because, instead of yangizing our food, they actually charge it with more yin, diffusive quality. Because of this we use gas or a more natural fuel. It is very difficult to be more healthy if you are using electricity all the time.

The second element used to yangize food is salt, which has an extremely contractive and preservative quality. We use sea salt because this has all the trace elements left after sea water has been evaporated in the sun.

It is very important that we learn to use salt carefully as it has a powerful effect on our condition. Too little salt can make us very tired and too much salt can make us rigid and tense. So experiment all the time with your salt intake because the amount you take is fundamental to your health.

Time and pressure are the other two yangizing processes used in making our food more life giving and digestible. Both these elements are used in pressing salads, pickling and pressure-cooking our main foods, our grains.

We use and adapt these four elements in cooking according to the season and time of day. In the morning and summer, yang times when energy is rising,we use less fire, salt, time and pressure in our cooking. In winter and evening, yin times of descending energy, we make more use of these four elements to balance with our environment.

Vegetable Cutting Styles

We use many different cutting styles, some of these in order to balance yin and yang in the vegetables and others for purely aesthetic reasons. Scientifically it has been proven that there is more sodium at the root of a vegetable and more potassium at the top of a vegetable; sodium is yang and potassium is yin. For this reason, one of the most frequently used cutting styles is on the diagonal; that is, cutting diagonally down the length of the vegetable. This cutting style opens up as much of the vegetable as possible to whatever cooking method you are using, it also balances the potassium, sodium content of the vegetable much more effectively than cutting on the round. Cutting vegetables in this way maintains a high charge, because each piece of vegetable contains within it a polarity between yin and yang, upward and downward energies. It is this charge we wish to take into our own bodies to nourish our life force. This life force is our greatest gift, so it is wonderful that here is a way for us to maintain and recreate our energies.

Cutting on the diagonal

Hold the knife diagonally along the length of the vegetable and cut diagonals of the same thickness. Use all the vegetable, because in its entirety each vegetable has life-giving energy, the top and tail especially so.

Cutting half moons

This style of cutting is often used for cutting onions but is suitable for cutting all round vegetables. We cut half-moons from shoot to root because then each piece of the vegetable contains a more balanced sodium/potassium ratio. Cut the onion in half lengthwise. Turn the half with the flat edge on the chopping board and cut thin or thick half moons depending on your cooking style.

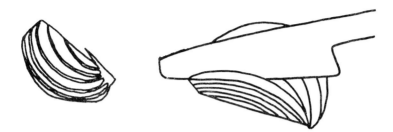

Cutting matchsticks

Cut the vegetable as you would for diagonals then pile the diagonals loosely one upon the other and cut through them lengthwise to create matchsticks.

Cutting wedges

For longer cooking styles such as stews and nishime this cutting style is ideal. Cut thick triangles by first cutting along the length of the vegetable diagonally with one stroke, and with the next cut diagonally in the opposite direction. This cutting style is really attractive.

9

Grains

Barley, wheat and oats have been traditionally grown and eaten in our climate; when properly cooked all of these are delicious grains and are very good for people living in England and Northern Europe.

Traditionally the macrobiotic diet emphasised the use of short grain organic, brown rice. Rice is a very healing grain. Here, in Europe, barley should be cooked with rice. If we eat rice on its own in this climate we cannot be happy because it is too heavy for us. Generally we use 20-30% pot or pearl barley with short or medium grain rice, particularly after practising macrobiotics for a number of years. Initially it might be quite appropriate for some people to eat mostly rice. In the macrobiotic way of eating we use short grain rice more in the summer. We will choose the grains we eat according to our individual condition. Initially it is best to approach a qualified macrobiotic dietary teacher for personal education.

To cook pot barley, wheat or oats with rice they should preferably be soaked overnight or precooked for 40 minutes before pressure cooking with the rice. Pearl barley needs to be soaked only 2-4 hours before being cooked with the rice.

In the winter we use more pressure cooked grain which warms our bodies more so we can balance with the cold outside. In the summer we tend to boil our grain slightly more often. For some conditions, boiling grain may be appropriate, even in winter.

Generally we pressure-cook for 45-50 minutes, timing from when the pressure comes up. Sometimes this can be a little shorter. To make a lighter grain in the spring or summer we can soak our grain for 2-4 hours before cooking it, and cook it for only forty minutes.

Other ways of making lighter rice for spring time and summer is to bring the rice to the boil before adding first salt and then the pressure- cooker lid; cook this rice a few minutes less than for regular pressure-cooked rice. When the rice has finished cooking and some pressure has come down naturally, let the rest out gently by raising the pressure valve slightly.

To make grain lighter use umeboshi plums or shiso leaves to cook the rice and barley. Depending on the needs of your condition, reduce the saltiness of the grain.

Because grains are so central to the diet it is important that you learn to cook them accurately as this will affect your entire health. Many people, at first, make the mistake of cooking their grains with too much water or not cooking them long enough, so please measure the amounts of water to grain, shown in the recipes carefully. When cooked, grains should not be soggy, rice should be broken open at one end but still retain its shape as a grain. If the grain is springy and chewy it has not been cooked enough to be easily digestible.

Pressure Cooked Rice.

1 cup of brown rice
1-1¼ cups of water
Pinch of sea salt

Using a stainless steel pressure cooker, wash the rice two or three times. Add the water and salt and bring up to pressure on a high flame. When the rice has reached pressure turn the flame very low and put a flame spreader underneath the rice. Cook at pressure for 45 minutes.

To bring the pressure down, either leave the rice to sit until the pressure comes down naturally, or, when the pressure has come about halfway down by itself, insert the end of a chopstick or spoon gently between the valve and the pressure cooker. This latter way of bringing the pressure down gives the rice a slightly lighter quality and more upward energy, ideal for spring and summer.

The rice should be taken out carefully, as soon as it has finished cooking, and put in a serving bowl. The grains of each spoonful should be gently separated before another spoonful is placed in the bowl.

Boiled Rice.

1 cup of brown rice
2 cups of water
Pinch of sea salt

Wash the rice carefully two or three times then add the water and salt and bring to the boil.

Turn the flame low and simmer gently for about 50 minutes until all the water is absorbed. For cooking rice in this way you need a pot with a tight fitting lid otherwise a lot of the water is lost as vapour.

Variations:-This rice makes a colourful salad when mixed with diced, boiled carrots, fresh corn and roasted sunflower seeds. Lightly boil cauliflower florets and red radish quarters then pickle them in umeboshi vinegar for about two hours. Drain the vegetables from the vinegar and add to the rice with some roasted pumpkin seeds.

Soft Rice.

1 cup of brown rice
5 cups of water
Pinch of sea salt

Wash and prepare the rice as you would for ordinary pressure cooked rice but when the rice has come to pressure, cook it for an hour instead of 45 minutes. This rice comes out very creamy and is excellent for breakfast or for people with poor digestion.

Variations:- Wash and cube pumpkin or carrot and cook this with the soft rice. This dish should still contain 80-85% rice.

At the end of cooking the soft rice, garnish with scallions or mix with finely chopped vegetable leftovers.

Rice variations

Rice is delicious cooked with beans and other grains or mixed with roasted chopped nuts and seeds at the end of cooking. Any rice and bean or grain mixture should always be at least 80-85% rice.

Rice with Beans.

When beans are cooked together with rice and barley the grain tastes a lot richer and more satisfying, it is particularly appropriate for winter.

Beans to be cooked with rice should either be soaked overnight or cooked 40 minutes before being added to the rice or barley. 60% rice, 20% barley and 15-20% beans makes a much lighter and more moving combination than just rice with beans, which can be a little heavy.

Beans can be cooked with barley, both having been soaked separately overnight. Barley and chestnuts, barley and lotus nuts, barley and black soya beans and barley and chickpeas all work well together.

Rice with Nuts and Seeds.

All nuts and seeds are dry roasted in a skillet, chopped and mixed in with the rice at the end of cooking. Sesame seeds, in particular, need sorting and washing in a sieve before roasting as all kinds of weird and wonderful extraneous bodies are to be found in a seemingly clean bag of sesame seeds.

You can, of course, roast nuts in the oven, but it is as well to know that by doing this, you are creating a much greater downward energy than you do when dry roasting on top of the cooker.

Variations:- Rice with walnuts, rice with almonds,rice with hazelnuts, rice with sesame seeds, rice with sunflower seeds, rice with pumpkin seeds.

Millet.

Millet is widely used throughout the world. Many people beginning macrobiotics associate it mainly with budgerigars and other exotic cage birds, lucky budgerigars! One of the nicest ways to eat millet is as a mould, cooked with vegetables. It then has a soft bread or cake-like quality and is excellent as a munch if you are trying to avoid flour products.

Millet and Chickpea Bread

This recipe makes a richer and more satisfying bread substitute than millet mould.

¼ cup of chickpeas
1½ cups of water
7" strip of kombu
1½ tsp. shoyu
2 spring onions sliced finely
2 cups of organic millet
5 cups of water
4 onions cut fine half-moons
2 pinches of sea salt

Wash and soak the chickpeas overnight.Place kombu at the bottom of a pressure cooker,then layer beans and water and pressure cook beans for 1¼ hours. Let the pressure come down, add shoyu and simmer for 30 minutes more. Grind the chickpeas in a suribachi (Japanese pestle and mortar) to a paste and mix in sliced spring onions.

Wash the millet in a sieve and dry roast it in a frying pan for about 10 minutes or until it releases a nutty fragrance.

Bring the water to the boil, add the sliced onions and simmer 5 minutes until the strong stinging quality has gone from the onions; add the millet and sea salt and turn the flame very low. Cook the millet over a flame tamer for 40-50 minutes until all the water has been absorbed.

Mix in the chickpeas and set for 1-2 hours or overnight in a bread tin or other square mould. Turn the chickpea and millet bread out and cut into slices.To heat before serving, the millet slices should be either fried or grilled.

Millet and Vegetable Mould.

1 cup of millet
2 onions sliced in half moons

Pinch of sea salt
3 cups of water

Bring the water to the boil, add the onions and boil them until they are transparent. Wash and drain the millet. Dry roast the millet in a frying pan until it releases a nutty smell. The millet will need to be turned a few times to prevent burning; it should not change its colour.Burnt food contains carbon which is not good for us and should not be eaten. Add the millet and salt to the onions and water. Turn the flame low, cover and cook for about 30 minutes until the water is absorbed. Choose a mould of the desired shape and rinse it in cold water. Pour in the millet and press it down well. Leave to set and cool for about two hours before returning out the millet and slicing it. Millet squares look very pretty garnished with parsley.

Variations:- Shoyu and ginger juice make a really nice seasoning for millet mould. Mix one teaspoon of shoyu and two teaspoons of ginger juice (grate fresh ginger root and squeeze it to extract the juice) and add to the millet mould about 5 minutes before the end of cooking stirring it in gently.

Miso and freshly ground mustard also make a good seasoning for millet mould but mustard, with its very strong fiery upward energy, is not suitable for everyone's condition. Miso and mustard can be added 5 minutes before the end of cooking in roughly the same proportions as shoyu and ginger.

All kinds of vegetables can be used either separately or together, especially carrot, celery, leek and cauliflower. For a light, summer dish brine pickled radishes and cauliflower can be cut into small pieces and mixed into the mould, at the end of cooking, with finely sliced scallions.

For a richer flavour vegetables can be sauteed in a half teaspoon of sesame oil, before adding them to the millet. Roast sunflower seeds or pumpkin seeds can be mixed into the millet at the end of cooking for a crunchy texture.

Soft Millet

1 cup of millet
4 cups of water
Pinch of sea salt

Cook this dish as you would the millet mould. It is a really nice breakfast dish, especially with chopped spring onions or watercress added in the last few minutes of cooking.

Millet and Lentil Balls.

1 cup of millet
⅓ cup of green lentils

4 cups of water
2 diced onions
2 pinches of sea salt

Boil the water and add the onion. Cook the onion until it is transparent and add the lentils, when they have been washed and sorted for stones and other foreign bodies.Simmer the onions and lentils on a medium flame for 30 minutes. Wash, drain and dry roast the millet and add this to the onions and lentils. Add the salt and simmer gently for 30 minutes until the water is absorbed. Allow the mixture to cool and either roll into little balls in your hands or make into patties and fry in sesame oil. Serve with a parsley garnish.

Variations:- Use aduki beans instead of lentils. Cook the adukis until they are about 70% cooked; this will be after about an hour and ten minutes. Add the millet and cook for 25 minutes. Add shoyu and ginger to season and cook ten minutes more, until all the water is absorbed.

Sweet Rice.

This is a more glutinous, protein rich rice than ordinary rice. It is not used as a main grain because it is too heavy in this climate. Generally it doesn't make good dessert because it is too heavy. Usually it is used as mochi which is described below. Initially, in the macrobiotic way of eating, mochi can satisfy a desire for baked desserts and so is a useful good quality substitute. Generally amasake or fruit and seed or nut desserts are better. For dessert recipes see **'Macrobiotic Desserts'** by the same author

Mochi.

1 cup of sweet rice
1½ cups of water
Pinch of salt

Pressure the sweet rice using the same procedures as for ordinary rice, or wash and soak the sweet rice for about six hours and pressure cook for only 30 minutes, with one cup of water to one cup of rice. Of these two methods of making mochi, I prefer the first, but do experiment and see which you find the better of the two.

When the rice is cooked, allow the pressure to come down naturally and place the rice in a suribachi (ceramic mortar) and pound it until the individual rice grains have broken and become really glutinous. This may take about an hour. As the mochi becomes more sticky dip the pounder in a little cold water occasionally to prevent sticking. A variation of mochi is half- pounded mochi, called ohagi. which is equally delicious, but not quite so strengthening. Pounding the sweet rice adds a great deal of yang energy to it, which is very vitalising.

Saute diced or minced carrots, onions or burdock and add ginger and shoyu to season about five minutes before the end of cooking. When all the moisture has been absorbed remove the vegetables to a bowl and allow them to cool. Mix the vegetables with the mochi which has been set aside to dry for a few hours. Drying the mochi slightly just makes it more easy to handle if you want to roll it into shapes or fry it. Wet your hands to prevent the mochi sticking to them, and either roll the mixture into balls and then in roasted sesame seeds, or dry roast patties in a skillet until the outsides are crisp.

Variations:- Saute finely chopped scallions with a little miso and water pureed together. Add the miso puree after the spring onions have been cooking for about two minutes, and continue cooking until all the moisture has been absorbed. Make the mochi into flat cakes, place the scallions in the centre and form into a ball with the scallions in the centre. Try this with other vegetables as well. These sort of surprises are good fun with everyone, children particularly enjoy them.

Sweet Mochi.

Sweet rice can also be pressure cooked with raisins, dried apple rings, hunza apricots or aduki beans and, after pounding, allowed to dry for a few hours and rolled into balls or little cakes as desserts.

Variations:- Nut creams blended with a little miso as seasoning are delicious in the centre of plain mochi balls. Roast 1/4 lb of walnuts, almonds or hazelnuts and grind them to a paste in a suribachi. Add about 1/2 a teaspoon of miso and mix with a little water, if necessary, to make a thick cream.

Cook aduki beans separately and add raisins. When the adukis are about 60% cooked, the addition of about 30% raisins makes them nice and sweet. Season with a pinch of salt when the adukis are 80% cooked. When all the water is absorbed mash the adukis and raisins in a suribachi to a paste. Roll the mochi into balls and cover with the aduki and raisin paste. If you like, place a roasted hazelnut or almond in the centre of the mochi ball and cut the ball open to serve. This can look very pretty.

Barley.

Barley has a lovely flavour and quite a lot of upward energy for a grain. It is rarely cooked as a main grain though because even when cooked it maintains a bouncy, chewy quality. Because of this barley is generally mixed with rice if it is to be eaten as a main grain. Barley is used much more often in soups and stews where it can be cooked for a longer time and harmonise with other ingredients.

All the barley we eat has had some of the bran layers removed, pearl barley is a more refined grain than pot barley. Pot is the more warming and vitalising of the two. Pearl barley needs less soaking time than pot barley. Hato mugi or wild barley can be bought from *"Clearspring", Old Street, London*, and is a delicious addition to rice. Hato mugi stew has also had one layer of bran removed and this grain can be cooked with rice without soaking it.

Barley Vegetable Stew.

1 cup of barley washed and soaked for two hours
½ cup of leeks
½ cup of carrots
¼ cup of parsnips
Dried tofu or seitan
4 cups of water
Oil
Shoyu

Saute the vegetables, add the barley and water and simmer for 50 minutes. Place cubes of seitan or dried tofu on top of the stew and cook for 20 minutes longer. Season the stew with shoyu to taste, 1-2 teaspoons should be enough, and cook for 20 minutes more.

Variations:- Almost any root vegetables are nice in barley stew, especially onions. Shiitake mushrooms are good too. Leafy green vegetables can be added, if desired, nearer the end of cooking. It is a good idea not to add too many vegetables and to try and create a simple harmonious flavour, perhaps three vegetables are ideal. Each vegetable has a different kind of energy and trying to blend too many different kinds of energy together in one dish only creates confusion. This confused energy becomes your energy when you eat the food, so cook simply and harmoniously.

Lentils are really excellent with barley in a stew. After the barley has been cooked for about 40 minutes add ⅓ cup of green lentils and cook for another 40 minutes. Add three onions, sliced in half moons, and layer them on top of the stew.Leave the lid of the cooking pot so that some of the stinging and more upward energy of the onions can be released. After about five minutes place the lid back on the pot and cook for 10 minutes. Add 1-2 teaspoons of shoyu to taste, two handfuls of finely chopped scallions and 2 teaspoons of ginger juice. Cook for 10 minutes and serve.

Soft Barley.

1 cup of barley
4 cups of water
Pinch of salt

Wash and soak the barley for a couple of hours before cooking. Bring the barley, water and salt to the boil and simmer on a low flame for 1-1½ hours. This is an excellent dish for breakfast. Serve with Gomasio or toasted nori strips.

Barley Salad

1 cup washed barley
1¾-2 cups of water
Pinch of salt

Wash and soak the barley for two hours. Combine barley, water and salt and bring them to the boil. Reduce to a low flame and simmer gently for one hour. Remove from the heat and toss the barley grains lightly. Replace the lid and let sit for 5 minutes.

Saute onion, carrot and celery or any other combination of vegetables and mix with the barley. Serve cold.

Oats

Whole Oat Porridge

1 cup of oats
5-6 cups of water
Pinch of salt

Wash the oats twice then the add water and salt. You can dry roast the oats first for a more nutty flavour. Bring the oats to the boil and simmer on a low flame for several hours. You can also pressure cook the oats for 1-1½ hours with four cups of water to one of oats. This makes a lovely creamy breakfast.

Rolled Oat Porridge

1 cup of rolled oats
2-3 cups of water
Pinch of salt

Use the oats either roasted or unroasted. Add the water and salt and bring to the boil. Simmer for thirty minutes on a low flame. Generally we prefer to use whole grains and just use oatflakes as an occasional variation. By the time the oats have been crushed through a roller they have lost their integrity as a seed, that is they have lost the energy that was in them that could create a new oat plant. Because the rolled oats have lost this life giving energy, when we eat them we do not absorb so much beneficial energy for living or healing ourselves. Too many oatflakes also create mucus in the body which then has to be eliminated in some way or another.

Wheat

Wheat is only occasionally used as a main grain; more usually it is cooked with other ingredients to make a grain salad. Wheat is, perhaps, most often used in the macrobiotic diet in the form of seitan. Seitan is an extraction of the wheat protein or gluten away from starch. We use the starch to thicken sauces, soups and stews, and cook the seitan with water, shoyu and ginger. Seitan is a delicious enriching food. It really loosens the body which may have got too tight from narrow eating, it is also strengthening and has a meat like texture for those who enjoy that quality in their food. We also use wheat in the form of wholewheat flour but we tend to avoid flour and flour products if we are trying to improve our health. This is because flour is difficult to digest, particularly in its baked form, and clogs the intestines causing stagnation and cloudy thinking.

Wheat Salad

1 cup of wheat berries
2 fresh corn cobs
½ cup of sunflower seeds
2-2½ cups of water
2 pinches of sea salt

Wash and soak the wheat berries in 1½ cups of water for about four hours. Place the wheat with the rest of the water and a pinch of salt in a pressure cooker and bring to pressure on a high flame. Turn the flame very low and pressure cook for 1¼ to 1½ hours. If there is any excess of water at the end of cooking this can be strained and saved for soup stocks. Place the wheat in a bowl and toss it gently to separate the grains. Boil a little water in a pan, add a pinch of salt. Cut the corn from the cob by slicing down the length of the cob; rotate the cob and repeat this slicing motion four times. Add the corn to the boiling water and after simmering for about five minutes. Strain the corn and reserve the water for soup stock. Mix the corn with the wheat. Dry roast the sunflower seeds over a medium flame until they turn to a light gold. Sunflower seeds need to be stirred frequently to prevent uneven cooking. Allow the wheat and corn to cool and mix in the sunflower seeds.

Wheat is also delicious used in its sprouted form. Sprouted wheat can be used for making salads. Simmer the sprouted wheat in boiling water for about 20 minutes, drain thoroughly and serve with a variety of boiled salad vegetables.

Wheat can also be sprouted and used to make bread. To sprout the wheat soak the wheat for at least 24 hours. In winter the soaking time might need to be longer as the temperature is lower. Drain the wheat and leave it covered with muslin or a bamboo mat, and rinse the wheat once or twice a day. The wheat will take 4-6 days to sprout, depending on the temperature of your house.

To make bread put the sprouted wheat through a grain mill. The consistency will be of a stiff granular dough. This dough can be mixed with different ingredients to make more interesting bread. Grated carrot or sprouted sunflower seeds can be added. For a sweeter taste, soaked raisins or grated apple can be added.

Place the dough in an oiled bread tin and press it down with a spoon. Put water to about ¾ inch in the bottom of a pressure cooker and place an upturned saucer inside the pressure cooker. Tie greaseproof paper over the bread tin and pressure steam for 1½ hours. This bread is lovely and sweet.

Seitan.

Seitan is a very good source of protein. It is easy to make and gives variety from using beans as a source of protein. Any wholewheat flour will make seitan but an 81% - 85% wholewheat mill is better because it contains less bran. Freshly milled flour produces a much better quality seitan. Using 1lb of flour, mix this to a dough consistency with cold water. Kneed the mixture for a few minutes and place it in a bowl with water to cover. Leave the dough mixture for at least 20 minutes. Take from the dough a lump which you can hold in your hands and kneed it under warm water; have a bowl of cold water handy also and transfer the dough alternately between the warm and cold water kneeding it all the time. Gradually the white starch will come out of the flour and the bran, leaving you holding an increasingly elastic piece of wheat gluten. The gluten is ready to cook when there is no more white starch coming from it and the gluten is smooth textured without a lot of bran in it.

Bring about 5 cups of water to the boil and add the gluten in about five balls. Simmer for five minutes and remove the seitan. Add a six inch piece of kombu to the water, having first wiped it clean of salt with a damp cloth. Add a tablespoon of shoyu and fresh ginger root cut into chunks. Put the seitan back in the water, either as balls or cut into cubes, and simmer for 30 minutes. The more gently you cook it the more tender the seitan becomes.

When cooked, seitan is delicious as it is, or sauteed with vegetables.

Buckwheat

Buckwheat is very high in calcium, vitamin B, iron and minerals but it is the most yang of the cereal grains and so should be eaten only occasionally. We generaly eat buckwheat either as a Kasha or buckwheat noodles.

Kasha with Onions

1 cup of buckwheat groats
2cups of boiling water
Pinch of sea salt
2 onions cut in half moons
½ teaspoon sesame oil

If the buckwheat is unroasted, wash and drain the groats and dry toast them in a skillet until they are nut brown. Add boiling water and salt to the pan and simmer on a low flame for 30 minutes. Place the groats in a serving dish. Heat the sesame oil in a frying pan and add the onions, saute the onions for 5 minutes and add a pinch of salt. If necessary add a little water to prevent burning and cover. Cook for two or three minutes more and mix the onions with the kasha. This dish is nice garnished with finely chopped scallions.

Noodles

To cook noodles place them in boiling water and add cold water. This helps the noodles cook more easily all the way through without becoming soggy. Simmer the noodles until they are done which will be about 15 minutes. To test whether they are cooked, take one noodle and slice through it. If the noodle is all one colour through to the centre then it is cooked.

Buckwheat Noodles

1 packet of buckwheat or soba noodles
Water to cover

Bring the water to the boil, there is no need for salt as the noodles are already salted. When the water is boiling, add the noodles and simmer until they are done. To test whether they are done, take one noodle out of the water and slice through it. If the noodle is one colour right through to the centr it is cooked. If the centre is a darker colour than the outside of the noodle, replace in the water and cook for 2-3 minutes more. Test the noodles again and if done, strain, and run them under cold water to separate. Buckwheat noodles have a lot of downward energy so a buckwheat recipe is not complete without some upward energy vegetables. Scallions go well with buckwheat as does watercress.

After boiling, noodles can be sauteed with vegetables. Try onions in half moons; saute until they are transparent, add fine carrot matchsticks, and saute two minutes more. Mince some watercress and place this on top of the onion and carrot. Add the cooked noodles and a couple of drops of shoyu. Put a lid on the skillet and cook for two minutes, then serve. A sesame seed or sunflower seed garnish is nice with this dish.

Soups

Generally we use soups as appetizers before a meal to get the digestion working, so that we absorb the rest of our food more effectively. For seasoning we use either miso or shoyu, except in grain soups where we choose to use salt as the seasoning so as to retain the lovely cream colour of millet or rice. We use miso and shoyu because they are both made with soya beans, fermented in salt over a long period of time. This fermentation process produces bacteria and enzymes which stimulate the digestion.

In making miso soups, ½-1 teaspoon of miso is used per person; the flavour of the soup should be strong, but not salty and the amount of liquid small in quantity, roughly a large cup of water per person is enough. We try not to take too much liquid as this tires the kidneys, which have to filter it, and dilutes and weakens the blood. One or two small bowls of soup and two or three small cups of bancha tea or grain coffee is plenty each day.

Generally shoyu and miso are added at the end of cooking. The flame is turned either very low or off, the miso is pureed in a little of the soup stock and added to the soup. The soup is allowed to sit for about five minutes so that the flavours have time to harmonise. Shoyu is usually added five minutes before the end of cooking and cooked with the soup.

Often, particularly with soups that have been cooked for a long time, a garnish is added to give some very light, upward energy to the soup. Creating this polarity between long cooking and a light garnish helps any dish move well through the body, makes it easier for the food to be assimulated into the body and means that we absorb from our food a more vitalised energy.

Soup Stocks

Kombu Stock
7" piece of kombu
5 cups of water
Wipe the kombu with a damp cloth to remove the salt and place the kombu at the bottom of a pot. Add the water, bring to the boil and simmer for about 5 minutes. Remove the kombu and save for re-use.

Shiitake Mushroom Stock
4 shiitakes
5 cups of water
Shiitake are dried mushrooms available from Oriental and good whole-food shops. Soak the shiitakes in one of the cups of water for a few minutes. Place the shiitakes, their soaking water and the other four cups of water, in a pot and bring them to the boil. Simmer for about ten minutes and remove the shiitakes.Save the shiitakes and use them in another dish. Usually shiitakes are soaked for about ten minutes and have their woody stems removed before being cooked.

Vegetable Stocks
The washed tops and roots of vegetables can make a lovely soup stock. Just boil the vegetables in 5-6 cups of water for ten miutes and strain off the vegetables. Save the vegetable ends for composting.

Grain Stock
Dry roast either rice, barley or millet until it becomes golden brown and releases a nutty smell. Boil the grain in 5 cups of water for ten minutes. Strain off the grain and keep it for making another soup stock or grain tea.

Bean Stock
The water left over from cooking chickpeas or aduki beans can be used to make a deliciously sweet soup stock.

Miso Soup
The main ingredient of miso is soya beans which contain 34% protein, nearly twice as much as meat or fish. Soya beans are also rich in calcium,phosphorus, iron, other minerals and lacithin. They contain all the amino acids essential to our diet, so it is really a good idea to use miso in soup every day. Miso can be added to any vegetable or fish and vegetable soup, but below I have written a few of the more healing and cleansing recipes. There are three different types of miso; Barley or mugi miso is used throughout the year and is made with barley koji. Rice or genmai miso is of a lighter quality than barley miso and is used in warmer, summer weather and hatcho miso is made with soya beans and is the heaviest and richest of the miso seasonings; it should only be used in cold weather and I think of it as being ideal to help the breath melt the cobwebby fingers Jack Frost trails across the windows at night when the cold makes him search out a warm bed to sleep in.

Onion Wakame Miso Soup

⅛ of a medium sized onion per person
A small strand of wakame washed and cut into 1" pieces
½ -1 tsp. of miso per person
1 large cup of water per person

Bring water to the boil and add onion. Simmer for a few minutes until the onion has become transparent then add the wakame and simmer for a few minutes more. Turn the flame off and puree the miso in a little of the soup water before mixing into the soup gently. Cover the soup and let it sit for about five minutes until the flavours have harmonised.

Daikon Miso Soup

1 cup of daikon matchsticks
5 cups of water
½ -1 tsp. of miso per cup of water
1 sheet of toasted nori cut into thin shreds

Bring the water to the boil, a vegetable or kombu stock is really nice in this soup, and add the daikon matchsticks. Simmer the daikon until it is tender and puree the miso in a little of the soup water. Turn off the flame and add the miso. Cover the soup and let sit for five minutes. Toast and shred the nori and use it as a garnish for the soup.

Pumpkin Kombu Miso Soup

½ a medium pumpkin skinned and cubed
1 diced onion
6" strip of kombu
½-1 tsp. miso per person
5 cups of water

Soak kombu for one hour in a little water and cut into 1" pieces. Add the pumpkin cubes to one cup of water and simmer for about 15 minutes then puree the pumpkin in a suribachi. Boil the rest of the water and add diced onion, simmering it untul transparent. Add the kombu, kombu soaking water and pumpkin and cook ingredients for a further 20 minutes. Turn of the flame and season with miso. Allow to stand for 5 minutes and serve the soup with a spring onion or watercress garnish.

Watercress Nori Soup

1 bunch watercress
5 cups of water
½-1tsp. miso per cup of water
1 sheet of nori toasted and shredded

Bring the water to the boil. Wash and cut the watercress into small pieces and add it to the water. Simmer the watercress for about two minutes. Puree the miso in a little soup water, turn off the flame and add the miso. Allow the soup to sit covered for five minutes. Toast the nori by holding a sheet, shiny side down, about ten inches above a flame for about 30 sesconds. To make sure the nori is evenly toasted move it in circles over the flame. Tear or cut the nori into shreds and use it to garnish the soup.

Grain Soups

Grain soups are especially good in cold weather although grains can be used as a base for soups throughout the year. Grain soups are a particularly nice way of using up left over grains. A lightly seasoned, grain soup makes a delicious breakfast.

Pearl Barley and Onion Soup

1 cup of pearl barley
6 cups of water
3 onions in thin half moons
½ -1 tsp. miso or shoyu per cup of water
1 sheet of toasted nori to garnish

Boil the pearl barley with the water for an hour. Saute the onions in ½tsp. of sesame oil, adding a little water if necessary, and cook them until they are sweet. Add the onions to the barley and cook for a further 10 minutes. Add shoyu and cook a further 10 minutes. Toast and shred the nori and use it as a garnish. A sprig of parsley is also good as an additional garnish to this soup to give it a lighter quality.

For pearl barley you can substitute hato mugi, a wild barley available at most oriental stores, which has a unique flavour.

Rice Shiitake Soup

2 cups of cooked rice
7" strip of kombu
1 diced onion
5 shiitake mushrooms
4 cups of water
2 tsp. of shoyu

Boil the kombu and shiitakes in the water for 10 minutes. Reserve the kombu for another dish or cut it into thin strips. Chop the stalks off the mushrooms and slice them into thin slivers. Add the onions to the soup stock and simmer them for a few minutes until they are transparent then add the rice, shiitakes and kombu and cook on a low flame for 30 minutes.

Add the shoyu and simmer for 10 minutes more. This soup really needs a garnish and either watercress or spring onions are delicious.

Variations:- rice, carrot cubes and leek, or rice onions and pumpkin.

Millet and Broccoli Soup

1 cup of cooked millet
3 large heads of broccoli cut fine
4 spring onions finely sliced
4 cups of water
2 tsp. shoyu
2 tbsp. ginger juice

Bring the water to the boil and add millet. Simmer the millet for about 20 minutes, add broccoli and cook on a low flame for 10 minutes. Add spring onions and shoyu and simmer for a further 10 minutes. Grate ginger and squeeze in the juice.

Variations:- Millet, carrot and onion, Millet, lentil and scallion, Millet, onion and celery, Millet,carrot and cauliflower.

Corn and Leek Soup

3 heads of corn
2 leeks cut finely
5 cups of water
2½ tsp. shoyu
Parsley and toasted nori to garnish

Cut corn from cob. Saute the leeks and corn for five minutes then add water and bring to the boil. Turn the flame low and simmer for 40 minutes. Season with shoyu and simmer a further 10 minutes. Add parsley and crushed toasted nori to garnish.

Variations:- corn and onion.

Bean Soups

Aduki Bean Soup

2 cups of cooked aduki beans
5 cups of water
3 carrots cut into half moons
1 parsnip cut into thick matchsticks

Place the adukis in the water and bring them to the boil then add the carrots and parsnips. Cook on a low flame for 30 minutes, add shoyu and cook the soup for 10 minutes more. Garnish with spring onions.

Variations:- Aduki beans, kombu and squash. Aduki beans onion and watercress. Ginger juice also adds an excellent flavour to aduki bean soup in any of its combinations.

Lentil Soup

2 cups of cooked lentils
2 diced carrots
1 thinly sliced celery stalk
4 cups of water
2 tsp. of shoyu

Bring the lentils and water to the boil and, adding the carrots, simmer for 10 minutes. Add the celery and cook for 10 minutes before adding the shoyu. Simmer the soup for a further 10 minutes and garnish with spring onions, watercress or parsley.

Split Pea Soup

1½ cups of green split peas
2 diced onions
3 stalks of celery diced
6 cups of water
½ cup of washed wakame
½ tsp. of salt

Layer onions, celery and split peas in a pot and gently add the water and a pinch of salt. Bring the peas to the boil and simmer for 45 minutes. Add the wakame, after slicing it into one inch pieces, and cook the soup for a further 20 minutes. If water evaporates, add more water to the desired consistency.

Beans

Beans are high in protein, carbo-
hydrates, iron and minerals;
many of them are rich in fats also. For improving our health it is best to
use the least oily of the beans and so, for general use, we include aduki
beans, chickpeas, whole lentils and black soya beans. Of these beans,
chickpeas are the most oily and therefore the richest; they can be used by
people who still crave, but are trying to avoid, dairy products and are a
very satisfying substitute. Of these beans, adukis have the most downward
or yang energy and are very good for healing and strengthening weak
kidneys. Even though yellow soya beans contain 34% protein, this protein
is not easily assimilable without fermentation and so we tend to eat soya
beans either as tempeh, natto or tofu, (which, although not fermented is
refined and the protein easily absorbed.)

Generally we cook beans for a longer time than many people. This is
because, if beans are not cooked until very soft, they are not easy to digest.
To aid in the digestion of beans we always cook them either with kombu
or wakame seaweed. The mineral rich seaweeds balance out the protein
and fat content of the beans.

There are three ways of cooking beans:-

1) Pressure cooking. Using 3 cups of water to one cup of beans,
pressure cook for 45 minutes. Take the pressure down, add salt or shoyu
to season and cook the beans uncovered, until all the water has been
absorbed. Pressure cooking is a very heavy or yang way of cooking beans
and, of the four varieties of beans mentioned above, we tend only to
pressure cook chickpeas.

2) Boiling. Boil one cup of beans to four cups of water for about 1½
hours or until they are about 80% done and add shoyu to taste. Cook 20
minutes longer until the water evaporates.

3) Shocking method. Add water to lightly cover one cup of beans.
Bring water to the boil and as the water is absorbed, pour more water
gently down the side of the saucepan to lightly cover the beans again.
Repeat this procedure until the beans are 80% done, add shoyu and
continue cooking until all the water is absorbed. With this method the
beans cook more quickly, but be careful not to let them burn.

Aduki Beans

7"strip of kombu
1 cup of adukis
Water
1 tsp. shoyu

Wash and sort the beans and, if you have time, soak them for a few hours. Wipe the salt off the kombu with a damp cloth and place kombu at the bottom of a pot, then add adukis and an amount of water depending which cooking method you are using (see above). When the beans are about 80% cooked add shoyu and cook the beans for about 20 minutes more.

A healing and strenghening way of preparing aduki beans is with 20% kombu and 10% vegetables. These percentages of seaweed and vegetables really help in the digestibility of the beans. The vegetables can be added about ½ way through cooking and carrot, onion, parsnip and squash are all delicious combinations.

Variations:- For a cold summer pate, puree the beans in a suribachi and add sauteed or lightly boiled vegetables and ginger juice. For a lighter dish vegetables with more upward energy can be combined with aduki beans, for example, celery, leeks or scallions combine well with aduki beans.

Aduki Kanten is also delicious and a light, spring or summer way of serving aduki beans. When the beans have nearly finished cooking, but still have a lot of juice left, add agar agar flakes, about 3 tablespoons of agar agar to one pint of water, and carry on cooking for at least 10 minutes or until the beans are thoroughly cooked. Wet a mould with cold water and sprinkle finely chopped scallions at the bottom of the mould. Spoon in about ⅓ of the adukis and another layer of scallions, Repeat this with the last third of the aduki beans making the bottom layer. This could also be done with very small carrot cubes which have first been sauteed in shoyu and ginger juice. Leave the mould to set for about two hours and turn it out onto a plate. Garnish with lightly boiled carrot flowers.

Lentils

Wash and sort the lentils. There are often small, lentil shaped stones among the lentils. Using 1 cup of lentils to 3 cups of water, bring the lentils to the boil and simmer for 45 minutes. Season with a teaspoon of shoyu and simmer for 10-15 minutes more.

A richer and yet slightly lighter way of cooking lentils is to take 3 onions, cut them into thin half moons and simmer them in some boiling water for 10-15 minutes before adding the lentils. The onions become really sweet. At the end of cooking stir in finely chopped scallions or parsley.

Lentils cooked with finely diced onion and celery, then pureed in a suribachi with about 50% leftover rice, can make nice little rice and lentil balls if garnished with parsley.

Chickpeas

Wash the chickpeas and pressure them, 1 cup of chickpeas to 3 cups of water for 1½ to 1¾ hours, with a 7" strip of kombu or the equivalent amount of wakame at the bottom of the pot.

After pressure cooking, drain the chickpeas from the juice saving both. Cut two onions in thin moons and saute in about ½ teaspoon of sesame oil. Wash and mince a bunch of parsley and add this to the onions after 5 minutes. Add enough of the chickpeas cooking water to just cover and add the chickpeas. For a variation, the chickpeas can be pureed before adding to the saute. Add a teaspoon of shoyu and simmer for about five minutes. To thicken add a teaspoon of Kuzu, which has first been diluted in a little cold water, and simmer for five minutes, stirring occasionally so that the kuzu mixes evenly.

Chickpea Dip

Mix one cup of cooked chickpeas with 2 diced sauteed onions and grind in a suribachi to a paste. Dilute 1 teaspoon umeboshi paste with a little water and mix with the chickpeas and onions. For a lighter flavour a teaspoon of lemon juice or rice vinegar can be added.

All sorts of vegetables would be nice in this dip. Carrots, parsnips, scallions and parsley combine particularly well with chickpeas and miso is really nice as a seasoning.

This is delicious as a spread on bread or crackers and if thinned with a little chickpea juice, it is a good sauce to pour over millet triangles or squares.

Lima Bean and Corn Kuzu

A delicious dish for light summery days. Cook lima beans by the standard boiling method of cooking beans, remembering to season with shoyu when they are 80% done. When the lima beans are cooked, mash them to a paste in a suribachi. To the cooked equivalent of one cup of dry beans, use three cobs of corn. Slice the corn from the cob and bring two cups of water to the boil with a pinch of salt. Boil the corn for 10 minutes then strain it from the cooking water and save both. Add the corn water slowly to the lima beans until you have a smooth runny sauce. Mix in the cooked corn and return to the heat. Mix a tablespoon of kuzu in a very little cold water and stir the kuzu into the lima bean sauce. Simmer for five minutes and prepare a mould by rinsing it with cold water. Pour the lima beans into the mould and leave to set for a few hours. The mould will be most effective if it is very shallow. Turn the mould out and garnish with chopped roast walnuts or almonds.

Chestnuts

We treat chestnuts as beans and cook them in a similar way using kombu. For dried chestnuts, soak them in water for at least two hours before cooking. Make sure you use the soaking water in the cooking as this contains much of the chestnut flavour and many nutrients. Cook the chestnuts as you would any other bean. They are delicious if thin onion half moons are added halfway through cooking. This mixture is delicious suribachied into a paste and used to stuff pumpkin, onion or cucumber which have been steamed. Chestnuts are delicious cooked alone and rolled into balls at the end of cooking.

Tofu

1 cup soya beans
7 cups water
1-1½ tsp. of nigari

Soak the soya beans overnight in two cups of water and grind through a blender or in a grain mill. Bring the rest of the water and the ground soya beans to the boil. When the water comes to the boil it rises very quickly. To prevent this sprinkle cold water on top of the soya milk and bring to the boil twice more. Using cheesecloth, strain the okara from the soya milk. Reheat the milk, after cooking the milk for about 7 minutes; it should be nearly boiling. Dilute the nigari in a little hot water but do not boil it. Add the nigari slowly to the soya milk and stir the soya milk very gently. The curd and whey should begin to separate and the water become a clear yellow, with pieces of tofu in it. Add only enough nigari to curdle the tofu, as too much makes the tofu taste bitter.

Strain off the tofu from the whey. The whey can be saved and used as a soap or shampoo. Turn the tofu into a holed box so that any remaining whey can drain out. The box should be lined with cheesecloth so that the tofu doesn't drain out through the holes as well! Cover the box with a press and place a weight on the press.

Tofu Recipes

Scrambled Tofu with Scallions

Place water to cover the bottom of a frying pan and add ½lb of tofu. Scramble the tofu on a medium flame for about 3 minutes, add 3 drops of shoyu and 2 scallions sliced finely. Cover and simmer for 3 minutes more. This dish is delicious served over noodles for breakfast. At the begining of the day we want a lot of upward or yin energy so this dish is lightly seasoned. Salt, shoyu and miso are yang and so have a lot of downward energy, so in the morning we use these seasonings more sparingly.

Fried Tofu

Tofu can be cut into small cubes and fried until golden brown. When the tofu is half done, a mixture of a third shoyu to two thirds ginger juice can be poured over the tofu and the tofu cooked until all the moisture is absorbed.

Alternatively the tofu can be fried until golden and then put on bamboo scewers with thin slivers of raw or blanched cucumber. A ginger shoyu dip can be made, again using one third shoyu to two thirds ginger juice and a little water.

Pieces of fried tofu can be added to stews or to nishime style at the end of cooking. They can also be put into soups or served on top of a vegetable saute.

Tofu Dip

½ lb. tofu
2 tbsp tahini
1 finely diced onion
½ -1 tsp. miso

The tofu can be used raw, which is more yin, or steamed for 5 minutes which creates a more yang energy to it. Blanch the onions in a little boiling water. Puree the tofu in a suribachi, together with the onion. Mix the tahini and miso with a little water to a light paste and puree with the tofu. Finely chopped scallions, ginger juice or lemon juice can be added for a lighter flavour. ½ a teaspoon of umeboshi paste can be substituted for the miso. Tofu is lovely with roasted ground nuts, particularly almonds, walnuts and hazelnuts. Add a little miso, shoyu or umeboshi paste to taste.

Tofu dressing can be made by adding more water to a tofu dip and is delicious over noodles or boiled salad.

Tofu Dumplings

½ lb. of tofu
Pinch of salt
Tbsp of kuzu
2 tbsp. of water

Drain tofu to remove moisture and mash in a suribachi. Mix the kuzu together with the water and add to the tofu with a pinch of salt and mix well. Make the mixture into small balls and place in soups at the end of cooking or on top of stews.

Variations:- The tofu can be mixed with any seasoning to make it more flavoursome, but the seasoning should be dry, otherwise the tofu becomes too wet to form dumplings. Tahini or sunflower spread are really tasty mixed in with the tofu, also mustard and miso.

Tofu made in this mixture is really nice as a stuffing for cabbage rolls. For this recipe finely chopped vegetables such as carrots or scallions can be added to the tofu mixture.Blanch the cabbage in boiling water and cut out the hard stem. Place the tofu at one end and roll the cabbage leaf into a packet, securing with a cocktail stick or wakame stem tied in a knot. Steam this mixture for about ten minutes, seasoning with shoyu and perhaps ginger.

Okara

Okara is the soya bean pulp left over from making tofu. It still contains a lot of protein and is really delicious. It should be cooked for at least 40 minutes before eating, as it is comparatively yin. It is good as a soup when cooked with some root vegetables such as carrot and parsnip.

Okara Saute

Lightly saute two onoins cut in half moons then add a cup of okara and saute in sesame oil for about five minutes. Add carrot and dried lotus root matchsticks and water to just cover the vegetables. Place a lid on the skillet and simmer for 30 minutes. Season with a teaspoon of shoyu and two teaspoons of ginger juice and simmer for a further 10 minutes.

Okara Burgers

2 cups of okara
1 carrot finely diced
1 onion finely diced
1 tsp. freshly ground mustard
Pinch of salt twice

Steam okara in a steamer for 30 minutes then remove it to a suribachi and mash it, with a pinch of salt, to a smooth paste. Saute first the onion then the carrot, adding a pinch of salt as you add the carrot to the saute. Mix the onion and carrot with the okara and form into patties. Fry the patties in a teaspoon of sesame oil until they are golden brown.

Seaweeds

Many people begining the macrobiotic diet find seaweeds the strangest part of our way of eating. We try to include them as a side dish about once every other day.

Slowly, as you learn to cook the seaweeds in many interesting ways, you will begin to find them an excellent addition to your diet. They are available from most wholefood shops.

Seaweeds are important in our diet because the contain iodine and lots of minerals. All of the edible seaweeds are rich in calcium, iron, vitamin A, vitamin C, niacin, iodine and other minerals. Seaweeds help to strengthen the intestines, liver, pancreas and sexual organs. Beacause of their high mineral charge they are able to draw toxins from, and cleanse the blood. If our blood is of a good quality then we are moving in the direction of health; so seaweeds are beneficial and it is important that we learn to enjoy them.

Wakame

Wakame is a light seaweed and has very versatile uses. It can be used in soups, bean stews, salads and cooked along with vegetables. It is delicious baked for 30 minutes, ground and sprinkled on grains as a condiment. It is a useful seaweed for helping discharge light dairy foods which have accumulated around the organs of the body.

Steamed Wakame with Ginger

Wash wakame under the tap and slice it into edible pieces, removing any hard, central strands you come across and saving them for soups, stews etc. Place wakame in a steamer over about half an inch of water. Bring the water to the boil and steam on a high flame for about five minutes. Grate ginger and squeeze a few drops of juice over the wakame. Add a few drops of shoyu, then replace the lid and cook for two minutes. This dish helps discharge accumulated animal fats and oils as well as eliminating salt from the body.

Steamed Green Beans with Wakame

Wash and slice green beans on the diagonal and place them on the bottom of a steamer. Wash and cut the wakame and place the wakame on top of the beans. Steam for about five minutes, add a few drops of shoyu and steam for 2 minutes longer.

Variations:- leeks and brussel sprouts, broccoli or cauliflower are delicious cooked with wakame.

Cucumber and Wakame Salad

Wash and slice cucumber finely. Soak the cucumber for an hour in about half a pint of water with a couple of pinches of salt. Wash and soak wakame for about ten minutes, until soft, and cut wakame into 1" pieces and mix wakame and cucumber together with a little rice vinegar, having first drained the cucumber from its soaking water. The cucumber is very pretty cut into matchsticks; thin slices of red radish pickled in umeboshi vinegar are also lovely against the dark green wakame.

Kombu

Kombu is a very strengthening seaweed, very good for the intestines and for breaking up animal fats and stagnation. We use it in many dishes, to add minerals to beans and vegetables and to make them more digestible. We also use kombu in soups and as a condiment over grain. A strip of kombu added to boiled vegetables brings out the sweetness in them without the need to use any salt.

When you buy kombu it is often grey and salt covered. Wipe the salt off with a damp cloth before using. Kombu is best soaked for 5-10 minutes before using. For using kombu in a dish of cooking time less than an hour, it is best to soak kombu for an hour before cooking with it. This makes it softer and more digestible.

Kombu Vegetable Rolls

These are an attractive way of serving vegetables. Cut carrots, parsnips or daikon (mouli) into round chunks. Wash and soak kombu and any long, thick wakame strands you have saved. Roll the kombu round the vegetable and tie with the wakame stem.

Place the rolls in a pot and half cover with the kombu soaking water. Bring the water to the boil and simmer for 30 minutes, adding a little more water if necessary. Add shoyu and simmer for 10 minutes more.

Variations:- You can do a mixed roll by quartering carrots, parsnip and burdock lengthwise. Take three of the quarters and roll them in kombu, tying at each end with wakamw stems.

Other vegetables including swede and turnips can be cut into rectangles and rolled in kombu.

Nori

Nori is the Japanese name for lava bread. Lava can be bought from a commercial grower, *'Clockie,'* in Scotland and is termed wild nori. This is lovely steamed with vegetables; Wild nori, carrot matchsticks and swede cubes, seasoned with shoyu and ginger. Alternatively wild nori and parsley makes a tasteful dish.

When you buy it, nori comes as a sheet. The simplest way of preparing this to eat is to hold the sheet, shiny side down, about 4" above the gas flame for about 30 seconds, moving the sheet in circular motion so that all parts are toasted. As they toast the colour changes from brown to a beautiful emerald green.

This sheet can be torn into strips to decorate soups and salads, used to cover rice balls or eaten just as it is. Toasted nori particularly helps the body clean itself of excess fruit and sugar.

Noodle Sushi

1 packet of udon or buckwheat noodles
1 bunch spring onions
5 sheets toasted nori
Rice vinegar

Wash and blanch the spring onions without cutting them and soak them in rice vinegar for one hour. Toast the sheets of nori and set them aside. Bring a pint of water to the boil and add the noodles. Most noodles are salted already, so there is no need to salt the water. Simmer the noodles until they are done, about 10 minutes. To test whether the noodles are cooked, take one noodle out of the water and cut it in half. If it is the same colour throughout the noodles are cooked, if the centre is still yellow return the noodle to the pot and cook for about two minutes before testing again. When the noodles are cooked strain them and set aside to cool. For this dish, if the noodles are sticky, all the better. When the noodles are cool lay a piece of nori on top of a bamboo mat. Layer the noodles onto the nori to cover the half closest to you. Place 3 or 4 spring onions in the centre of the noodles and roll the nori around the noodles tightly. Cut into 1" sections.

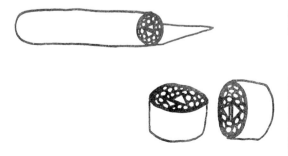
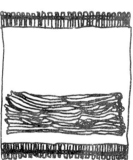

Arame

Arame seems to be the most immediately attractive of all the seaweeds to the unaccustomed seaweed eater. If cooked well it has a sweet and delicate flavour.

It is necessary to soak both arame and hijiki for five minutes before cuuting and cooking. After soaking cut criss cross through the pile of soaked arame to make 1" squares. Arame and hijiki expand a lot when soaked, so only a small amount taken from your seaweed packet will go a long way.

Arame with Onion

1 handful of dry arame
2 onions diced
1 tsp. sesame oil
½-1 tsp. of shoyu

Oil a lidded frying pan and when the oil is hot place the arame in the frying pan and saute for about 3 minutes. Add the arame soaking water to just cover the arame and simmer for 20 minutes. Layer the onion on top of the arame without mixing and add more water if necessary. Simmer for 20 minutes and add shoyu to taste, simmering again for 10 minutes. When the arame has finished cooking all the water should have been absorbed. Mix the onion and arame together gently with a pair of chopsticks and serve.

Variations:- Arame and carrot matchsticks, arame and roast chopped nuts, arame and roast sesame seeds.

Hijiki

Hijiki has the strongest flavour among the seaweeds and the greatest downward energy. It is particularly rich in calcium, having 16 times as much as milk per unit measure.

Hijiki is prepared for cooking in the same way as arame and is delicious with onions and carrots as arame is. Hijiki is thicker than arame and needs about 10 minutes more cooking time.

Hijiki Tofu Salad

½ cup of hijiki
½ cup of sesame seeds
2 carrots as matchsticks
1lb soft tofu
1½ tsp. miso
1 tsp. toasted sesame oil

Wash and soak the hijiki for 10 minutes. Strain and keep the soaking water. Cut the hijiki into one inch lengths.

Brush enough sesame oil to lightly cover the bottom of the pan and, when hot, add the hijiki. Saute the hijiki for about five minutes, add soaking water, cover with a lid and cook 10 minutes more. Add the carrot matchsticks on top of the hijiki so they retain their lovely orange colour and saute a further ten minutes. Add a little shoyu to taste.

Bring three cups of water to the boil and add the tofu. Simmer the tofu for five minutes, strain the tofu and squeeze to rid the tofu of excess moisture. Mash the tofu in a suribachi with the sesame seeds and miso. For a lighter taste use the same amount of umeboshi paste in place of the miso. When the hijiki and carrot have cooled, combine with the tofu mixture and serve cold.

Hijiki Rolls

2 cups of cooked hijiki
2 carrots as matchsticks
½ tsp. of sesame oil

Pastry

1 cup of small oat flakes
1 cup finely milled wh / wh flour
5 tbsp corn oil
Pinch of salt
Water to mix

Saute the carrot matchsticks, after 3 minutes add a few drops of shoyu and a few drops of ginger juice and saute 2 minutes more. Set aside. Mix the flour and oatflakes with the oil and salt. Slowly mix in water to make a dough consistency and leave for about ½ an hour before rolling it out into a thin rectangle about 9" by 7". Place a layer of hijiki on the pastry dough and then a layer of carrots and roll into a cylinder. Seal the edges. Bake in a medium oven for about 30 minutes. Allow to cool and slice into 1" pieces.

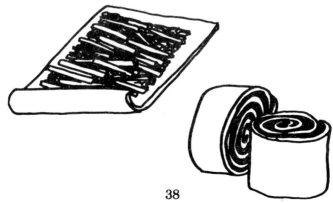

Vegetables

W hen we think about the energy of different vegetables we divide them into three categories; root vegetables, round vegetables and leafy, green vegetables.

Yang moves downwards toward the centre of the earth. Yin moves upwards towards the sky. Vegetables which are more developed in a downward direction i.e. root vegetables are more yang. We eat these for their gathering, strengthening effect  because yang is a gathering force giving centreness, direction and will-power to the personality. Those vegetables which are formed fairly equally of yin and yang we call round vegetables. They have a certain amount of upward energy like cabbage which grows above the ground but it curls back upon itself with the force of the yang, downward energy. We eat these vegetables for harmonious reflections but if we eat only this type of vegetable we lack within ourselves the dynamic polarity, which the more yin and yang vegetables give us.

Yin vegetables are those which grow up and out like celery,spring onions, kale, swiss chard and watercress. Their main growth is in a stretching upwards towards the sky. We eat these vegetables in order to feed ourselves with their yin energy which is that of flexibility, light heartedness, laughter and imagination.

So we must not eat exclusively upward or downward energy vegetables but eat them in harmony to create health. Generally in spring and summer we eat more yin vegetables; 60% leafy greens and 40% root vegetables and in winter more root vegetables.

In macrobiotic cooking we do not use citrus fruits, except the occasional addition of lemon rind or juice to add lightness and movement to a dish. Many people ask where we get our vitamin C from. This is a needless wory. Many vegetables contain far more vitamin C per unit measure than citrus fruits, for example:-

Citrus fruits	38-61 mg	per 100 grms
Broccoli	113 mg	per 100grms
Cabbage	47 mg	per 100 grms
Kale	125-186 mg	per 100 grms
Watercress	79 mg	per 100 grms
Cauliflower	78 mg	per 100 grms

The other mineral people think they may lack in a macrobiotic diet is calcium which they think is only contained in large quantities of cow's milk. Again there is nothing to worry about as many vegetables and seeds contain more calcium per unit measure than milk, for example:-

Cow's milk	100-118 mg	per 100 grms
Watercress	90 mg	per 100 grms
Parsley	200 mg	per 100 grms
Radish greens	190 mg	per 100 grms

Boiling

We boil our vegetables between 1 and 5 minutes. We use very quick boiling to make boiled salads, which are a very delicious, light way to take upward energy without the more dispersing effects of raw foods.

For boiled salad you can use almost any vegetable and almost any cutting style as long as it isn't too chunky. A variation of cutting styles is pretty in a boiled salad. We usually use two, three or more vegetables in this cooking style with an eye to colour, texture and shape contrast. If you cook your vegetables whole and cut them afterwards, they have a sweeter flavour. Of course this isn't always possible. Finely cut vegetables should be cooked for about 1 minute, thickly cut vegetables should be cooked about 3 minutes.

Broccoli and Carrot Flower Salad

Boil carrot flowers for two minutes, strain them and run under a cold tap to prevent further cooking and to retain their brightness and colour. For a different taste, carrot can then be marinated in rice vinegar for an hour.

Cut the broccoli floret away from the stem and boil for about two minutes. Rinse under a cold tap and mix with the carrot flowers.

Save the boiling water for soups stocks and stews, it is full of minerals. Save the broccoli stalk and any other bits of unused vegetables for pickling or making soup stocks. We should try not to waste any food which we bring into our kitchen, but think of all the different kinds of energy that went into the making of it, the earth's energy, the sun's energy and the energy of the person who planted and harvested our food.

Variations:- Cauliflower, cucumber matchsticks and radish flower boiled salad. Leek, parsley and celery boiled salad with sunflower seeds. Carrot and daikon matchsticks with sesame seeds.

Wakame Onion and Carrot

1 handful of dried wakame
2 onions diced
1 carrot as matchsticks

Rinse the wakame under a cold tap to remove excess salt and set aside. Bring to the boil enough water to just cover the onion and carrot then add the chopped onion to the water and simmer until it is transparent. Add wakame chopped into 1" pieces and the carrot matchsticks and boil together for about 10 minutes, covering with a lid. Add shoyu and simmer 5 minutes more. Strain the vegetables and wakame and arrange them attractively. Either save the remaining water for soup stock, or add some kuzu and a teaspoon of ginger juice and serve as a sauce over the vegetables.

Carrots with Sesame Miso

5 carrots quartered
Pinch of salt
½ cup of sesame seeds
1 tsp. genmai or mugi miso

Bring to the boil enough water to cover the carrots and boil the carrots for five minutes then strain. Dry roast the sesame seeds and grind them finely in the suribachi and add the miso and a little of the carrot cooking water to make a sauce. Arrange the carrots decoratively, pour the sauce over them and garnish with a little raw or blanched parsley.

Variations:- Sesame miso sauce can be lovely with many boiled or sauteed vegetables. Scallions or leeks or watercress are delicious but need a slightly shorter cooking time, so experiment with these.

Sauteeing

There are three different kinds of saute; short, long and water saute. Water saute is very useful for people who have been recomended to reduce their oil intake to the minimum and who still like a rich taste in their cooking. In a short saute we are trying to create a lot of upward energy, we cook our vegetables from yang to yin so the vegetables retain lightness. Layer the most yang vegetables on the bottom and saute these one or two

41

minutes before adding the lighter vegetables.A good example is onion and chinese cabbage quick saute.

For long saute we add the lightest vegetables first and the root vegetables last. There are two exceptions to this; burdock and onion. When using either of these vegetables in a saute they must be cooked 2-3 minutes alone first before the other vegetables are added. This is because both, although yang vegetables, contain a strong yin element which cooking alone eliminates.If other vegetables were cooked with onions from the begining of cooking it would be impossible to rid the dish you are making of that strong yin quality, because the other vegetables would absorb it.

Carrot and Parsnip Matchsticks

3 carrot matchsticks
2 parsnip
1 tsp. sesame oil
Pinch of sea salt
3 drops of shoyu

Heat sesame oil in a skillet over a medium flame, add the carrots and saute them for a minute, then add the parsnip. Sprinkle over a pinch of salt and cover. Saute for 10 minutes adding a little water if necessary. Season with shoyu and cook 2 minutes more.

Onion and Chinese Cabbage

1 onion cut in half moons
6 chinese cabbage leaves
3 drops of shoyu

This dish is deliciously sweet. Heat a teaspoon of sesame oil in a pan over a medium flame and add the onion. Saute the onion until it is transparent. Cut the cabbage leaves along the diagonal into thin strips and layer on top of the onion. Cover the pan and saute for 2 minutes. Add the shoyu and saute for two minutes more.

Variations:- This recipe is good with squares of tofu added on top of the chinese cabbage, also thin strips of seitan. Ginger also adds a nice touch of life to this dish.

Try also onion and carrot, leek and chinese cabbage, cauliflower, carrot and scallions.

A sweet and sour sauce can be made with the addition of a tablespoon of rice vinegar when you are using vegetables like onion and chinese cabbage, which have a natural tendency to become sweet. There is no need to add any sweetener, but you might like to add a very small amount of barley malt with the rice vinegar to get that sweet and sour taste.

Carrot and Almond Nitsuke

3 carrots cut in matchsticks
10 almonds
1 tsp. sesame oil
3 drops shoyu

Wash and cut the carrots. Heat the sesame oil in a skillet and add the carrots. Saute the carrots for about five minutes, add the shoyu and saute for two minutes more. Dry roast the almonds and chop them lenghtwise into quarters. Serve the carrot and sprinkle the almond over the carrot. A little ginger juice can be nice in this dish, grate ginger and add a teaspoon of ginger juice at the same time as the shoyu.

Water Saute

Onion and Carrot Top Water Saute

2 onions haf moons
A handful of carrot tops
½ tsp. of shoyu

Place enough water in a skillet to just cover the bottom and bring to the boil. Add the onions and simmer until they are transparent. Add the carrot tops which have been washed and finely chopped. Cover the pan and simmer for five minutes. Add either shoyu or miso and cook for 2 minutes more. This dish is delicious served on its own or with roasted seeds, particularly sesame or pumpkin seed.

Try your own variations of this water saute; cabbage is really nice in combination with a little rice vinegar and shoyu; leeks are tasty with a little umeboshi paste for seasoning. Mix the the paste with a little water before pouring it over the leek. Watercress water saute is delicious made into a sauce with a little kuzu at the end of cooking. This can be poured over millet squares or fried tofu squares.

Broccoli and Carrot Long Saute

3 carrots quartered
2 broccoli stems and heads
1 tsp. of sesame oil

For a long saute, vegetables can be cut larger. Wash and halve the broccoli lengthwise. Heat the oil in a skillet and saute the broccoli for 3 minutes, add the carrots and cover. Cook on a medium flame for 20-25 minutes adding a little more water if necessary. Season with a few drops of shoyu and covering again saute for 3 minutes more.

Variations:- Seitan or tofu can be added to this dish in the last five minutes of cooking. When using tofu a little ginger juice is a particularly nice seasoning.

Almost any vegetables are good in a long saute, but it is best to use vegetables which hold together well. Most round and root vegetables will be good for this dish and celery also.

Steaming

Steaming is a gentle way of cooking vegetables, but quite strengthening. Mostly we use steaming to cook greens, this style of cooking is particularly good for the lungs.

The way to steam is to place your washed and cut vegetables in a steamer and cover the bottom of the pot with about half an inch of water. Cooking on a high flame steam the vegetables for 5 minutes, add a few drops of shoyu and steam for 2 minutes more before serving.

If you don't have a vegetable steamer you can place a quarter inch of water in the bottom of the pan, add the vegetables and bring to the boil. Turn the flame to medium and steam the vegetables for about 7 minutes.

Kale, broccoli, cabbage, cauliflower, spring onions, leeks, radish greens and chinese cabbage are all lovely prepared in this way.

For steaming onions, a longer cooking time will be needed. Using the same method, steam onions for between 15 and 20 minutes. After 15 minutes sprinkle a drop of shoyu in the centre of each onion, cover and steam five minutes longer.

Any water remaining from cooking the onions can be made into a kuzu sauce by diluting a teaspoon or more of kuzu in a little cold water and cooking it for about five minutes with the onion water. A great variety of seasonings can be used for this sauce, finely chopped parsley, scallions or watercress are all delicious. Either mustard or ginger add a fine hot taste and rice vinegar a sharp sweet flavour. Roasted chopped nuts or seeds also blend excellently.

Nishime

This style of cooking is otherwise known as waterless cooking as it is done with as little water as possible.

1 cauliflower head quartered
2 carrots cut in chunks
7" strip of kombu
Water to cover bottom layer of vegetables
½ tsp. shoyu

Wipe excess salt off the kombu with a damp cloth and soak the kombu in cold water for one hour. Wash and cut the vegetables into chunky pieces using any cutting style you like, but making sure they are all of similar size. Layer the vegetables with the lightest or most yin vegetables at the bottom and the most yang vegetables at the top. This dish makes good practice for you in deciding which vegetable is which. Compare them for compactness which is a yang characteristic, and for their water content which is a yin characteristic.

Layer the soaked kombu at the bottom of the pot and add the vegetables from yin to yang over it. If you are taking a moderate amount of salt in your diet sprinkle a pinch of salt on the top layer of vegetables, if you are trying to reduce your salt intake this is not necessary. Add the kombu soaking water to cover the first layer of vegetables. Cover the pot and bring to the boil on a high flame, reduce the flame to medium and simmer the nishime for 25 minutes. Add shoyu and simmer for 10 minutes more then serve. Cut the kombu seaweed into 1" squares and decorate the nishime with the kombu.

You have to be quite careful with this dish as it is an easy one to burn. Check it halfway through cooking and if it seems to need more water pour a little down the edge of the saucepan. At the end of cooking, all the water should have been absorbed by the vegetables.

This is a very satisfying and strengthening style of cooking but has quite a downward energy to it, so we use it about three times a week.

For a richer variation add dried tofu, mochi balls or seitan on top of the vegetables.

Pressure Cooking Vegetables

Sometimes we pressure cook vegetables, but not very often as there is a lot of downward energy in this style of cooking. Usually we pressure cook our grains which makes them more strengthening and so we tend to cook our vegetables more lightly to make a balance.

Two similar vegetable dishes can be made by using the pressure cooker; these are onion and carrot butter. These two dishes have a very strong gathering energy, so they would be used in small quantity in a meal, either as a stuffing, spread or garnish.

Cover the bottom of a pressure cooker with quartered onions or carrots and water to nearly cover. Pressure cook for 30 minutes, strain off any extra juice and save this for soup stocks. Mash the vegetables to butter consistency in a suribachi and add a little miso to taste. A few chopped scallions could be added to lighten the dish.

Kinpira

4 carrots as matchsticks
1 burdock root as matchsticks
2 tsp. toasted sesame oil
2 tsp. shoyu

2 tbsp. roasted sesame seeds

Wash and cut the carrots and burdock. Heat a large frying pan and add oil. Heat oil and saute burdock on its own until the strong smell burdock releases, when it is first cooked, has gone. Place the carrot matchsticks on top of the burdock and cook uncovered for 5-7 minutes, adding shoyu halfway through cooking.

When cooked, kinpira should be sweet tasting and slightly crisp. Wash, sort and dry roast sesame seeds in a frying pan over aa medium flame until the seeds crush easily between the thumb and third finger. The seeds should remain the same colour. If the seeds pop out of the pan then the flame is too high. Mix the roasted sesame seeds with the carrot and burdock and place it in a serving bowl.

Pickles

There is no need to buy vegetables especially for pickling as there always seems to be so many left over pieces of vegetables. Keep discarded cauliflower greens, broccoli stems and old vegetables; cut them into attrctive shapes and pickle them.

If you have a garden, at certain times of the year you will be inundated with a particular vegetable. Rather than using freezing to preserve your vegetables, which destroys a lot of their nutritional value, pickle your vegetables because this enhances their nutritional value.

Pickling changes the sugar in vegetables into lactic acid which aids digestion and strengthens the stomach and intestines. Eat a few pieces of pickle at the end of a meal each day and you will feel a change in your energy level; it will be much better.

There are so many different types of pickle. I shall explain some of the simpler and more commonly used types of pickle here.

Brine Pickle

Boil 1 pint of water with 1 teaspoon of salt and allow to cool. Wash a suitably sized jam jar and allow to dry. Collect together your unused vegetable pieces and cut them into similar sizes but any shape that attracts you. It is best not to bottle more than three different types of vegetable together in one jar as too many different energys mingled together creates confusion. The smaller you cut your vegetable pieces, the quicker the pickle will be ready to eat. If you are pickling very watery vegetables, such as cucumber, you can cut it to the size required and srpead the pieces to dry for about a day before pickling.

Put the pieces of vegetable into the jam jar and cover with brine. Seal the jar and store it in a cool dark place. In winter the pickle should be ready in 1-2 weeks, in summer it can take as little as three days. Check your pickles every day as sometimes scum developes on the surface.If this happens just scoop this surface off with a spoon, otherwise it will taint the pickles.

For variation in flavour and quality you can add pieces of ginger root, small pieces of kombu, celery or dill seeds.

Salt Pickles

3lb of chinese cabbage
⅛ cup of sea salt

Wash and cut the cabbage leaves then spread them out to dry for a day. Layer the cabbage in a ceramic container with a layer of salt on the bottom, then a layer of chinese cabbage and salt, alternating until you finish by covering the last layer of chinese cabbage with salt. Place a lid or plate on the crock and press down with a weight, this could be a large stone or jar of water. Cover with cheesecloth and store in a cool dark place for two weeks or longer.

Wash and perhaps soak the pickles for about ½ an hour before serving to reduce their salt content. Ordinary white cabbage, daikon (mouli) and carrot can also be good.

Shoyu Pickles

This kind of pickle is especially good with root vegetables; sliced carrot, swede, turnip or daikon into matchsticks.

Mix equal amounts of shoyu and water and, placing vegetables in a jar, add the shoyu water to cover. Leave this pickle for between 6 hours and 2 weeks depending on the kind of pickle that you want. Again, if these pickles develope a scum, skim it off immediately so that it does not taint the pickle.

Sauces and Dressings

Kuzu Sauce

1-1½ cups of vegetable water
1 tbsp. of kuzu

Kuzu is a very good quality thickening agent; it is made from the root of a plant which grows on the side of mountains. It is this strong, hardy nature we absorb as we use kuzu in our cooking. Kuzu relaxes and soothes the whole digestive tract.

Mix kuzu with cold water and leave it to stand a couple of minutes before adding to the vegetable water. Mix the diluted kuzu with the vegetable water and bring to the boil, reduce the flame to low and simmer for 5 minutes after adding a few drops of shoyu.

There are many, many variations that you can make to this sauce; a little ginger juice, ground mustard or lemon juice can be added. Roasted or ground nuts or seeds can be mixed in with kuzu sauce, pumpkin and sunflower seeds are particularly nice sprinkled on top of the sauce. Watercress, parsley, scallions or finely diced carrots can be cooked in the vegetable water for a few minutes before the addition of the kuzu. Purees of many vegetables such as, squash, carrot, onion or chestnut can be mixed with the vegetable water before adding a little kuzu. The variations are almost as endless as your imagination - experiment and see!

Kuzu sauce is lovely over steamed onion or leek. Cauliflower and walnut kuzu sauce go well together.

Tofu Sauce

Boil or steam tofu as a block for about five minutes. It is fine to use tofu raw but the quality is quite different, it is much more yin and less digestible. Mash the tofu in a suribachi and add a little shoyu and tahini to taste. Add water to make the desired consistency. Instead of adding shoyu it is possible to make a more salty taste by mixing a little umeboshi paste with water or suing sauerkraut juice or soup stock. Seitan cooking water would also add a nice flavour.

Variations:- Tofu, miso and ground walnuts or almonds. Tofu, shoyu and lemon juice.

Chickpea Sauce

Cook chickpeas until they are very soft as recommended in thebeans recipes. Saute onion half moons in a little sesame oil. Transfer the chickpeas to a suribachi and grind them, having reserved any cooking juice that has not been absorbed. Add the onions and mash them into the chickpeas. Wash and chop scallions finely and mix in. Blend a teaspoon of umeboshi paste with any extra cooking water and blend this into the chickpeas to make a sauce of the desired consistency. A little lemon juice can be added if your health is good.

This sauce is delicious over millet mould squares or saute vegetables.

Miso, Sesame Spread or Dressing

Mix 1 part miso with 3 or 4 parts of roasted, ground sesame seeds and add water to make the desired consistency. Variations include miso and walnut spread, or miso and almond spread.

Umeboshi Dressing

2 tsp. of umeboshi paste
½ a cup of water
¼ tsp. of grated onion or ginger

Puree the umeboshi, and onion or ginger in the suribachi and gradually mix in the water. This dressing is good over boiled, pressed or noodle salad.

Rice Vinegar and Shoyu Dressing

3 tbsp. of rice vinegar
1 tsp. of shoyu

Mix and serve over salad or steamed vegetables.

Ginger Juice and Shoyu Dressing

3 tsp. ginger juice
2 tsp. of water
1 tsp. of shoyu

This dressing is delicious with many recipes. It is very good as a dip used in breaking up oily foods so that they are more digestible. For this reason this recipe is often used as a dip or sauce for deep fried food, tempura style cooking and fish. It is also a lovely dip for mochi balls and is delicious over salads.

Condiments

Condiments should be used sparingly as they are generally salty. A little condiment is medicinal and beneficial to our health, a lot is certainly detrimental. It is best to take only one condiment with each meal and it should be realized that, for the most part, they are a very yang factor in the diet.

Gomasio

12 tsp. sesmae seeds
1 tsp. of sea salt

Sort, wash and roast the sesmae seeds over a gentle flame so that they retain their original colour. To test whether they are done, rub the seeds gently between the thumb and fourth finger. If the seed breaks open they are done. Transfer the sesame seeds to a suribachi and grind them gently and patiently in a circular motion until they are about 40% ground. Quickly roast the salt then add it to the sesame seeds and grind them together until the seeds are 80% ground.

This is a good way of taking salt, because oil helps in the digestion of minerals and the salt becomes covered with the sesame oil. Keep gomasio in a sealed jar and take about 1 teaspoon each day. Gomasio keeps fresh for about a week and should be remade frequently.

For children of 2 and over, who need far less salt than adults do, 20 tsp. of sesame seeds to 1 of salt is about the right proportion, and a third to a half tsp. a day. Children under 2 should not be given gomasio, or much salt in cooking, as too much salt can make them very unhappy and stunted in growth.

Miso Scallion Condiment

1 cup of chopped scallions
1 tbsp. of miso
1 tbsp. of water
1 tsp. of sesame oil

Saute scallilons in oil. Puree miso with water and add to the scallions. Cook on a low flame until all the moisture is absorbed. This dish is cooked only occasionally as it is very salty. It is a good condiment to eat on top of rice. There are other miso condiments such as carrot top and parsley miso condiment

Nori Condiment

1 sheet of nori
1 tsp. of shoyu
Water to cover

Tear the sheet of nori into little pieces and place it in a pan with enough water to just cover. Leave the nori for 8 minutes before cooking so that it can absorb the water. Simmer the nori for between 5 and 7 minutes, then add the shoyu and cook for 2 minutes more. This condiment helps the body discharge toxins, depending on your condition take between ½ and 1 teaspoon of condiment each day.

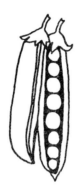

Desserts

Generally we eat desserts between two and three times a week. In the summer we eat more fresh fruit desserts and in the winter more grain based desserts cooked with dried fruit. Barley malt and rice syrup are used as sweeteners because they are a grain based sugar. Honey and sugar are far too extreme foods and are to be avoided for health and happiness.

Often sweeteners do not need to be used at all, particularly if dried fruits are used. These become particularly sweet if cooked for a long time, especially dried apples, hunza apricots and raisins or sultanas.

Alexia Raisin Polenta
¼ lb alexia raisins
1 large cup of cornmeal
Pinch of salt
3 cups of water

Rinse the alexia raisins and cook them in 1 cup of water with a pinch of salt for 30 minutes. We always add a pinch of salt to fruit, as the addition of mineral neutralizes the acidic nature of fruit and makes it more digestible and sweeter. Take the raisins off the flame and mix in the cornmeal. Add the remaining two cups of water slowly, stirring so that the cornmeal doesn't lump. Place the cornmeal back on the heat, turning the flame very low and cook for about 30-40 minutes. Stir the polenta frequently as it burns easily.

When the polenta is ready, either pour it into a mould, or serve it into individual dessert glasses and garnish with roasted, chopped almonds or walnuts. Hunza apricots are also delicious with polenta and should be cooked for at least 40 minutes, de-stoned and then mixed with the cornmeal.

Apple and Apricot Parfait
9 apple rings
9 hunza apricots
5 cups of water
2 pinches of salt
2 tbsp. of kuzu

Place apple rings in a pot with a pinch of salt and 2 cups of water. Bring to the boil and simmer gently for 30 minutes. If necessary add a little more water to the apples so there is a syrup. Mix one tablespoon of kuzu with a little cold water and add this to the apples. Cook the apples and kuzu gently for a further five minutes.

Pour the apple kuzu to half fill dessert glasses and rest these on their sides until the kuzu sets. Cook the hunza apricots in exactly the same way as the apple rings except use three cups of water and simmer them for 50 minutes before adding the kuzu.

When cooked, pour the hunzas over the apple kuzu in the dessert glasses and top with chopped nuts or tofu cream.

Oat, Dandelion Coffee and Walnut Mould

2 cups of oat flakes (medium)
4 tbsp. dandelion coffee
4 cups of water
Pinch of salt
¼ lb roasted walnuts
1 tbsp. barley malt (optional)

Boil the dandelion coffee in the water for 10 minutes then strain off the dandelion coffee and save it to use in another recipe. Allow the water to cool and add the oats and a pinch of salt. Simmer the oats for 20-30 minutes until it makes a thick porridge. Wet a mould with cold water and, at the bottom, arrange a layer of roasted walnuts. Pour in half the oats and add another layer of walnuts. Add the rest of the oats and press a layer of walnuts into the top of the mould. Allow the mould to cool for about 2 hours then turn it out onto a plate.

If you like a sweet taste in your dessert, heat 1 or 2 tablespoons of barley malt with 3 tablespoons of water until it has dissolved. Add a teaspoon of ginger juice and pour this mixture, when it has cooled a little, over the mould.

Pear and Blackberry Kanten

1 pear
1 cup of blackberries
1 tbsp. of rice syrup
3 tbsp. of agar agar
Pinch of salt

Wash and slice the pear. Bring a pint of water to the boil with the pear and a pinch of salt. Simmer the pear pieces for 2-3 minutes then remove them and arrange the pear slices decoratively at the bottom of a wet mould. Add the agar agar to the boiling water and stir until it dissolves. Wash the blackberries in a sieve and add them to the water. Simmer the blackberries for about 15 minutes. At the end of cooking add the rice syrup and stir until it has dissolved. If the rice syrup is cooked for any time it loses its sweetness. Pour the blackberries and water over the pears in the wet mould and allow to cool for two hours before turning it out. Fruit kanten is really nice served with something a little crunchy, sliced roast almonds or oats roasted with barley malt.

Chestnut Dessert

1 cup of dried chestnuts
3 cups of water
1 piece of kombu
1 tbsp. of kuzu
Pinch of salt

Soak the dried chestnuts for about 2 hours. Wipe the salt off the kombu with a damp cloth and place it at the bottom of a pot. Pour in the chestnuts and the chestnut soaking water. Bring the chestnuts to the boil and simmer them with a well fitting lid. As the water evaporates, add another cup of water. Repeat this 2 or 3 times. The chestnuts should take about one and a half hours to cook. When they are 80% done add a pinch of salt and 2 more cups of water. When the chestnuts are cooked remove them from any remaining water and save the water. Take the kombu out and save it for using in another dish. Mash the chestnuts in a suribachi and add the cooking water gradually to make a smooth paste. Return the chestnut puree to the heat and if it is too thin mix kuzu with cold water and stir it in. Simmer for 5 minutes.

Pour the chestnuts into dessert glasses and garnish with something either tangy or bitter. Try some finely grated ginger or lemon peel, roasted sesame seeds or walnuts.

Beverages

Bancha Tea

Bancha tea is our regular daily drink. There are now several types of bancha tea available in natural food stores including green tea, usual bancha tea and bancha stem tea. Bancha stem tea is also commonly known as kukicha. All come from the same tea bush, green tea is made from the leaves harvested in summer, bancha from dried leaves harvested in the autumn and kukicha from the branches and stems of the tea bush which are then dry roasted. Green tea is the most yin and can help discharge the toxic effects of eating animal foods, however bancha stem tea is our usual beverage and contains plenty of calcium, iron, vitamin A and C, as well as protein and other minerals.

Bancha is made by adding one tablespoon of bancha to one pint of water, bringing the water to the boil and simmering it for about five minutes. Pour through a bamboo strainer into individual cups.

Keep the bancha twigs to re-use. They can be used 4 or 5 times and then, either a little more tea can be added, or the original twigs discarded. It is good to buy a pot just for keeping bancha tea in, we use a Pyrex glass jug which can be heated. This is useful because you can tell at a glance, by observing the colour of the tea, whether it is ready to drink or not.

Grain Tea

Dry roast brown rice, pot barley or pearl barley over a medium flame for about ten minutes, stirring quite often to prevent burning. Boil two tablespoons of roasted grain to one and a half pints of water, simmering for ten minutes or so.

Yannoh Grain Coffee

3 cups of brown rice   *2½ cups of wheat*
1½ cups of aduki beans   *2 cups of chickpeas*
1 cup of chicory root

Wash and dry roast all ingredients separately in a skillet until they are dark brown, stirring frequently to prevent burning. Mix together and grind to a powder or grist in a grain mill. The easiest way to prepare yannoh is to use a coffee percolator that goes on the stove. Use one tablespoon of yannoh to one cup of water, it can be used several times. Simmer on a low flame for 5-10 minutes.

Meal and Menu Ideas

Breakfast

Of course it is good to have a variety of foods for breakfast. It is a good idea not to eat any foods that are too heavy to be easily digested, as these tend to stop us thinking. So light foods are ideal for breakfast, particularly boiled salad and pickles. If you crave richness, scrambled tofu is a quick and very light breakfast.

Gradually it becomes easier to eat less and les at breakfast, particularly if we are not doing hard physical work. It is much easier to think quickly and plan an interesting day ahead on an empty stomach. When we are empty physically it is easier to give out on an emotional and intellectual level.

We tend not to eat fruit or jam at breakfast as these foods, like sugar, are strong yin and make the day more dispersed. A salty start to the day is not such a good idea either as it tends to make us more tired and weary throughout the day. This is the reason why we do not eat marmite and other such breakfast spreads. If we like to have a salty taste at breakfast time miso soup is the best way to have salt.

Often people like to have a creamy breakfast. Whole oats make a lovely creamy breakfast. They can be washed, soaked and cooked about 20 minutes last thing at night. Whole oats then take only 30-50 minutes to cook in the morning.

Often when people first come to the macrobiotic way of eating they want a milk substitute. Soya milk seems the obvious answer. Soya milk is fatty and indigestible and needs to be cooked with minerals to be digestible. There are a few brands of soya milk such as Bonsoy and Edensoy which are good quality soya milk and taste better too. A small quantity of these is not harmful to the health, but drunk daily, as a replacement for milk, soya milk is not good for adults or children.

Lunches

Lunches should be quite light and easily digestible because if you are healthy you will have so many things you want to do with the rest of the day, that you will not wish to be debilitated by too heavy meal.

Fried rice and vegetables, seasoned with a little shoyu, is a good lunch. Noodles, topped with vegetables in kuzu sauce, or in a miso soup with other vegetables, makes a light, very easily digested lunch. Left over grains can be made into balls and rolled inroast, ground sesmae seeds for a quick lunch. Pickles are always good at the end of your meal to help digest your food.

In the winter it is good to have something warm for lunch. Grain miso and vegetable soup is a light way of eating enough food to keep us going until a more substantial meal at dinner.

If you like richer food at lunch time, tofu can be steamed quickly with vegetables, shoyu and, sometimes, a little ginger. You can buy already prepared protein foods such as smoked tofu, dried mochi, dried tofu, and seitan. Some of these foods are ready to eat and some take 10-30 minutes to prepare. Mostly these foods have directions for use on the packet. You can always try to locate a cook in your area who regularly uses these foods and learn more from him or her about interesting recipe ideas.

Dinner

In the evening it is fine to eat a more elaborate meal. Of course this depends on the time you have available to cook it, but at least every other evening it is good to make something a little richer and more unusual, so that you are taking a variety of different energies in your diet.

We often begin an evening meal with soup. For our main course we eat 50-60% grain, a root vegetable dish such as nishime, a greens dish, such as a boiled salad and either a bean dish or a seaweed dish.Two or three times a week have a fresh or dried fruit dessert. Kantens and kuzus are the quickest to make.

Below, I have suggested a few dinner menus. I include some dinner menus which need to be adjusted to the time of year and to each persons condition.

In general I am trying to present some interesting menu ideas. Each person will cook each dish differently and so it is impossible to convey accurately how to make a balanced meal in writing. The best way to learn this is to join a class given by a more experienced teacher.

Monday
Miso soup with fresh daikon and finely chopped daikon greens
Pressure cooked rice, pot barley and aduki beans
Nishime brussel sprouts
Steamed wakame, carrot and sesame seeds
Blanched spring greens and white cabbage salad with rice vinegar
Tuesday
Shiitake shoyu broth with spring onions
Boiled short grain rice with pearl barley
Seitan, leek and onion stew with seitan cooking stock
Quick saute carrot matchsticks with shoyu
Hijiki and red radish flower salad
Wednesday
Onion and wakame miso soup with parsley garnish
Millet and cauliflower chickpea bread
Boiled carrot triangles with ginger and shoyu
Long saute cauliflower greens
Daikon ume vinegar pickles
Thursday
Corn and leek shoyu broth
Pressure cooked long grain rice with sunflower seeds
Onion and carrot matchstick long saute with sauercraut
Cabbage and tofu rolls
Wakame, spring onion and red radish salad
Friday
Miso soup with green beans and carrots
Pressure cooked short grain rice with wheat
Aduki bean and spring onion kanten
Nishime burdock, onion and broccoli
Boiled kale
Saturday
Barley, onion and parsley soup with toasted nori garnish
Pressure cooked rice with red radish, corn and parsley boiled salad
Steamed spring greens with tofu and sunflower dressing
Carrot and burdock short saute
Celery pressed salad marinated in ginger and shoyu
Sunday
Watercress and kombu miso soup
Boiled rice and pot barley
Arame onion and black sesame seeds
Baked parsnip
Steamed chinese cabbage and bok choy
Radish flower quick pickles in rice vinegar

59

What to Buy First

When we first find out about the macrobiotic way of eating there seems a vast array of foods we are not familiar with and so I would like to help you with suggestions for the most useful *'first buys'* that will give you enough variety for a weeks menu, but will not leave you too much out of pocket.

GRAINS
Organic short grain brown rice
Organic pot and pearl barley
Organic wheat
Organic whole oats
100% wholewheat noodles

PROTEIN
Aduki Beans
Chickpeas
Lentils
Seitan
Sweet rice

VEGETABLES
A variety of root, round and leafy green vegetables in season and preferably organic;particularly carrots, onions, kale or spring greens, broccoli, cauliflower, watercress and parsley.

SEAWEEDS
Wakame
Kombu
Arame
Agar agar

SEASONINGS
Shoyu soya sauce
Sea salt
Barley miso
Rice vinegar
Fresh ginger root

SNACKS
Pickles
Tamari roasted sunflower seeds

BEVERAGES
Brancha or three year twig tea
Barleycup

Food Suppliers

If you have any problems buying any of the foods used in this book, they can be obtained by mail order from:-

Clearspring Natural Grocer
196 Old Street
London EC1V 9BP Telephone: 071 250 1708
They also supply foods wholesale, so you may be able to get your local health or wholefood shop to stock them.

Classes

Classes on macrobiotic cooking and individual dietary guidance are given by a number of teachers and centres in Great Britain, Ireland and Europe. For a full list write to:-

The Commumity Health Foundation
188 Old Street
London EC1V 9BP Telephone: 071 251 4076

Other Books Published by Cornish Connection

Introduction to Macrobiotics, Oliver Cowmeadow
A clear and simple introduction to the macrobiotic approach to a healthier way of eating and living. 30 pages, £1.95

Macrobiotic Desserts, Michele Cowmeadow
Over 80 sugar and dairy free recipes using simple and wholesome ingredients like fruits, nuts, seeds, grains and natural sweeteners to create delicious puddings, cakes, cookies and pies. 48 pages, £2.50

Yin and Yang. A Practical Guide to Eating a Balanced and Healthy Diet, Oliver Cowmeadow
A clear and practical guide on how the ancient system of yin and yang can be used to design a diet for greater health, prevention of sickness and a balanced and positive mind. 80 pages, £3.95

Food: Nature's Energy Creates You, Peta Jane Gulliver
Explains how the seasons affect us and the energies of foods, and how we can eat seasonal foods including many wild plants for beter health. With over 70 recipes. 98 pages, £4.95

These books can be ordered from your local bookshop, or obtained directly from the address below. Please add 10% to your order for post and package. Please enquire for details of wholesale terms.

Cornish Connection, The Coach House, Buckyette Farm, Littlohompston, Thtnes, Devon TQ9 6ND Telephone: (0804 26) 593

Index to Recipes

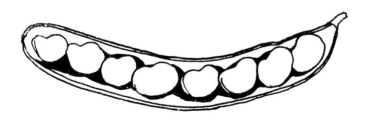